A is for Anxiety

is for

A Primer for Parenting through the Apocalypse

Words by Kate Brennan
Illustrations by Cameron Austin Brown

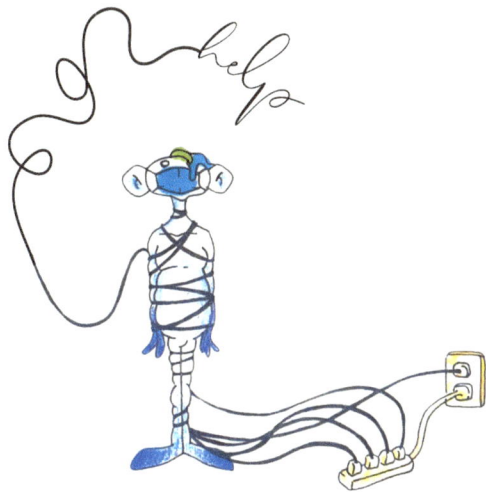

A is for Anxiety

Abortion-ban,

Anti-Vax.

D is for Deception and Delta and the Demagogues who Drove it.

E is for Earthquakes Everywhere

Earth Exhausted

as our host.

F is for Fire, Flood, and Famine

and Fear on either coast.

G is for Global warming,

Gaslighting,

Gluttony.

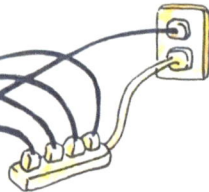

I is for **I**nsurrection, **I**nflation, **I**mmunity and **I**CU.

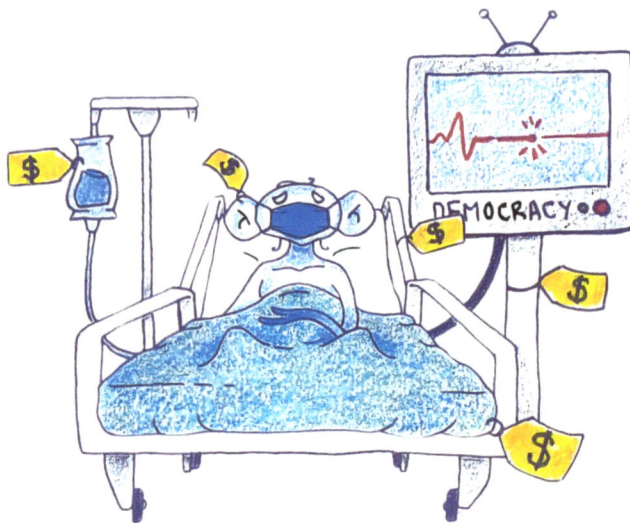

J is for the **J**uggernaut of **J**ustice

and

JUST

GET THE

JAB,

WILL YOU?!

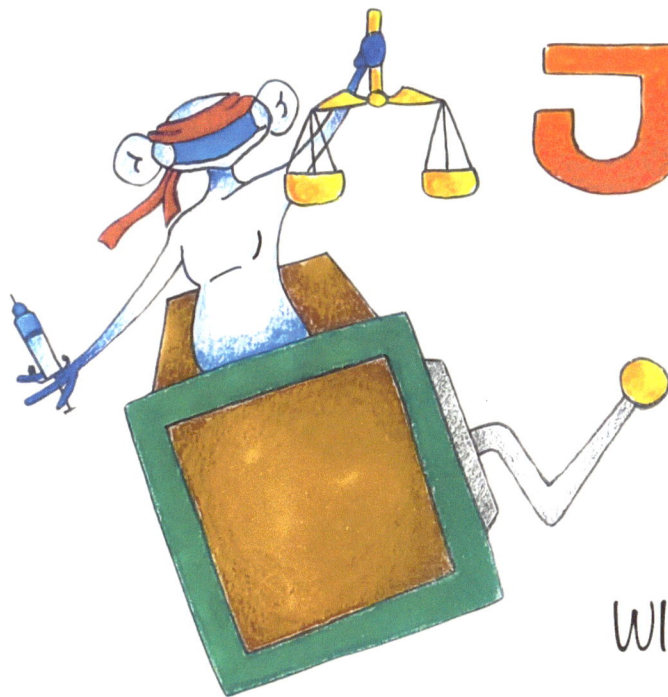

K is for **K**indness and

Keeping - **K**eeping on,

Keeping safe,

Keeping sane.

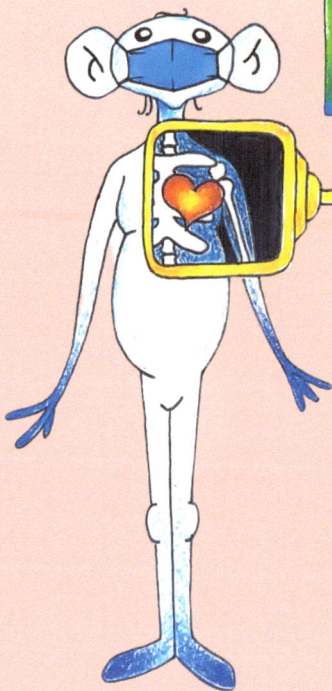

L is for Languishing, Losing-

Losing Life, Losing sleep,

Leaving Lanes.

M is for **M**ask up,

MeToo,

Mitigating risk,

Meiosis

WELL, THIS WON'T END POORLY!

N is for

Nasal Swabs,

New Strains,

and

Needling

Nasty

Neurosis.

O is for Omicron, Obsessing,

Outdoors,

....Out of Our wits.

P is for Pandemic, Patience, and Pushing Parents Past their limits.

Q is for Q'Anon,
Questioning,
Quitting,
Quarantine.

ASK AGAIN LATER!

R is for Remote

Life, School, Work, Therapy...

S is for

School **S**hootings, **S**ystemic Racism,

Misogyny

T is for **T**esting,

T O R N A D O E S !!

T- Cells

and

Technology

U is for **U**nemployment,

Universities,

Ukraine,

and the **U**nknown...

UNKNOWN

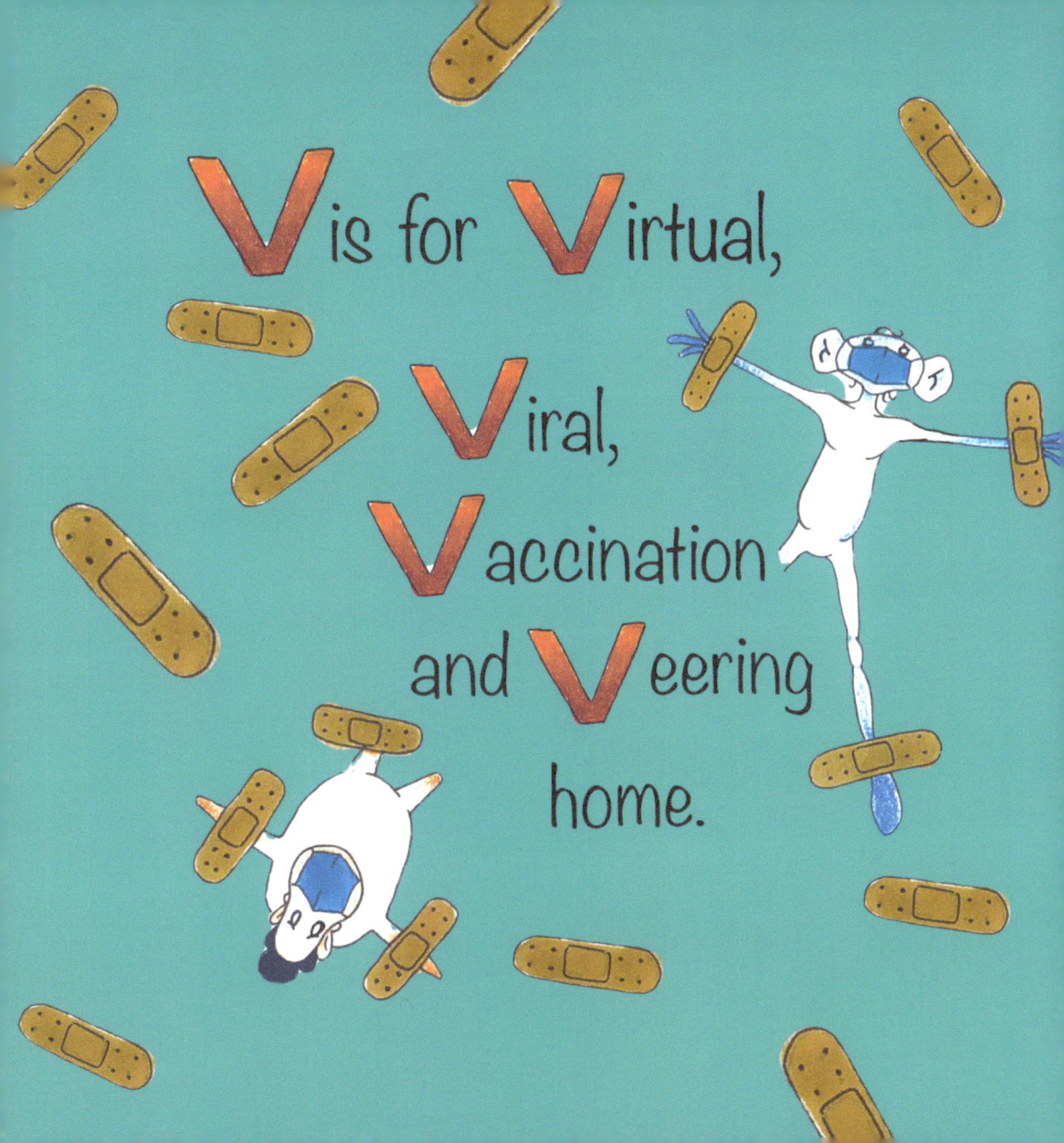

V is for **V**irtual,
Viral,
Vaccination
and **V**eering
home.

W is for **W**eary **W**omen
Wrenched from **W**retched **W**ork

X is for

feeling **X**enacious

and for **X**enaphobic jerks.

Y is for **Y**ard work and **Y**elling

Yearning for **Y**ears

through the gloom.

and finally, but not surprisingly,

Z of course is...

Zoom!

Kate Brennan (words) is an artist-educator-creator & mom with work in McSweeney's, Slackjaw, Belladonna, Jane Austen's Wastebasket, Frazzled & more. Her plays and musicals have been produced across the country. She was named a Jonathan Larson Grant Finalist for Visionaries in Musical Theatre & a Finalist for the Cultural Alliance Innovator Award.

You can read more on her Substack, More Humor More Humanity.

● ● ●

Cameron Austin Brown (illustrations) is an actor, poet, visual artist, and songwriter based in Chicago. His poetry and illustrations have been published in Oklahoma City University's The Scarab. He recently completed his debut collection of poetry and illustrations, Emotional Oranges.

As a Black man and a member of the LGBTQIA+ community, his work amplifies the experience of young people who struggle to find community in a static world.

Sending love &
encouragement to parents
& children everywhere.